The *Hot or Not* Quiz for Couples

The Sexy Game of Naughty Questions and Revealing Answers

J.R. James

All rights reserved. No portion of this book may be reproduced in any form without permission from the publisher, except as permitted by U.S. copyright law.

This book is for entertainment purposes only. This book is not intended, nor should the reader consider it, to be relational advice for any situation. The author makes no representations or warranties with respect to accuracy, fitness, completeness, or applicability of the contents of this book.

Copyright © 2020 Love & Desire Press

Written by J.R. James

All rights reserved.

ISBN 13: 978-1-952328-08-4 (paperback)

Spice up your love life even more, and explore all the discussion books for couples by J.R. James:

Love and Relationship Books for Couples

Would You Rather...? The Romantic Conversation Game for Couples (Love and Romance Edition)

Sexy Game Books for Couples

Would You Rather...? The Naughty Conversation Game for Couples (Hot and Sexy Edition)

Truth or Dare? The Sexy Game of Naughty Choices (Hot and Wild Edition)

Never Have I Ever... An Exciting and Sexy Game for Adults (Hot and Dirty Edition)

The Hot or Not Quiz for Couples: The Sexy Game of Naughty Questions and Revealing Answers

Pillow Talk: The Sexy Game of Naughty Trivia Questions for Couples

The Naughty Newlywed Game: A Sexy Game of Questions for Couples

Sexy Discussion Books for Couples

Let's Talk Sexy: Essential Conversation Starters to Explore Your Lover's Secret Desires and Transform Your Sex Life

All **THREE** *Let's Talk About...* sexy question books in one massive volume for one low price. Save now!

Let's Talk About... Sexual Fantasies and Desires: Questions and Conversation Starters for Couples Exploring Their Sexual Interests

Let's Talk About... Non-Monogamy: Questions and Conversation Starters for Couples Exploring Open Relationships, Swinging, or Polyamory

Let's Talk About... Kinks and Fetishes: Questions and Conversation Starters for Couples Exploring Their Sexual Wild Side

Change your sex life forever through the power of sexy fun with your spouse, partner, or lover!

www.sexygamesforcouples.com

Sexy Vacations for Couples
https://geni.us/Passion

HOW TO PLAY THE GAME

The rules for this game are very simple:

There needs to be at least two people to play. It's a great game for new couples to learn about each other, or couples who've been together a while to test how well they know their partner.

On each page there are quiz questions. You and your partner can either go through the quiz taking turns asking one another the questions, or you can play the game explained below:

One player reads the question in its entirety to the other player. The player reading the question can then guess what the other player will answer. For example: Tim and Lisa are playing together. Tim reads,

"Where do you like to be kissed?" Tim knows Lisa likes her neck kissed, so that's what he guesses her answer would be. Lisa agrees that's her favorite spot, so Tim gets a point. (You can use anything to keep score.) Lisa then gets to guess what Tim's answer to the question would be and has the chance to earn a point as well. After ten questions, there is a prize page. **Whoever has the most correct guesses and the highest score is the winner of the round and wins the prize.** It's a game that rewards how well you know your partner! The player with the lower score needs to follow the directions on the prize page to reward the winner. (In the event of a tie for the round, then **both** players must award the prize to one another.) After the prize is completed, reset the scores and start a new round.

As you spend time discussing the answers,

you'll soon you'll find yourselves smiling, laughing, and enjoying the sexually charged conversation. Who knows? You may even discover new sexual possibilities for your relationship.

Just have fun, because as long as you're enjoying time with your partner and sexy conversation, you both win!

ROUND 1

1
Where on your body do you like to be massaged?

2
What music gets you in the mood?

3
What's the hottest sex position in your opinion?

4

Do you prefer to dominate or submit in bed?

5

Nude sunbathing: Hot or not?

6

What's hotter: Trying to have sex quietly so you don't get caught, or having a quickie at an unusual time of day?

7
Where do you like to be kissed?

8
Drunk sex: Hot or not?

9

Would you rather give a lap dance or receive one?

10

What parts of your body do you like bitten or sucked?

Prize Page

The winner of this round gets to choose what the loser has to wear, or not wear, for the next three rounds.

ROUND 2

11
What physical trait of yours are you most proud of?

12

What's your idea of an erotic date?

13

Which movies or TV shows can get you in the mood?

__14__
Is sex with someone you just met hot, or not?

__15__
What's sexier to you, humor, intelligence, or good looks?

__16__
What's one of your sexual fantasies?

__17__
What's your favorite time of day for sex?

18

What's one kink or fetish you'd like to try?

19
Which would you prefer: Oral or anal sex?

20
What's one part of your body that embarrasses you?

Prize Page

The loser has to try and make the winner moan in pleasure within two minutes. You can do it in whatever way you think will work the quickest.

ROUND 3

21
Do you have a favorite sex toy?

22
Threesomes: Hot or not?

23
Where's your favorite place to have sex?

24
What's your favorite sexy song?

25
What's the quickest way to get you into bed?

26

What's a turn-on of yours that you don't like to talk about?

27
Strip clubs: Hot or not?

28
What's one of your biggest turn-offs?

_29_

Are you more attracted to people older or younger than yourself?

_30_

What part of someone's body catches your attention first?

Prize Page

The winner of this round gets a sexy striptease and lap dance from the loser. The winner gets to pick out the song they have to dance to.

ROUND 4

31
Do you like being tied up or handcuffed?

_32_

Who is one celebrity you'd sleep with if given the chance?

_33_

What's the most sexually daring thing you've ever done?

34
Is there anything you'd never do in bed?

35
Is swimming in the nude sexy?

36
What do you like to wear to bed?

37
What makes you feel sexy?

38
Where on your body are you ticklish?

39
What are three things you find sexy in a person?

40
How do you feel about hotel sex?

Prize Page

The loser of this round needs to softly tease the winner's chest, neck, and ears with their lips and tongue for one minute.

ROUND 5

_41_
Do you like to be vocal during sex?

42

If we were to roleplay, what role would you like to play?

43

Is there any part of your body that is "off-limits?"

44

Have you ever been, or would you ever be, naked in public?

45

Butt stuff: Hot or not?

46
Where is one place you'd never have sex?

47
What is one profession you find super sexy?

48
What do you like your partner to wear for a sexy evening?

49
Sex in a hot tub: Hot or not?

50
Have you ever watched another couple have sex?

Prize Page

The winner of this round gets to pick any part of their body and have the loser sensually and seductively kiss it for two minutes.

ROUND 6

51
What's your idea of great foreplay?

52
Would you strip and give a lap dance to someone for the right amount of money?

53

Do you consider yourself a sexual person?

54

Sex in vehicles: Hot or not?

55
What would you like to do better in the bedroom?

56
What makes for hotter sex, physical attraction or emotional connection?

57
Where would you go to take a sexy or erotic vacation?

58
How do you feel about BDSM?

59
Do you find sexting a turn-on?

60

Would you play strip poker (or other strip game) in a group setting?

Prize Page

The winner of this round gets to choose a food item, place it anywhere on their body, and have the loser lick it off of them. (The winner can switch roles if they so choose, and lick it off of the loser instead.)

ROUND 7

61
How do you feel about posing for nude photos?

62
Orgies: Hot or not?

63
Would you let someone watch you masturbate?

64
Do you like dirty talk?

65
How do you feel about anal play?

66

Would you have sex outside? If so, where?

67

Would you ever make a private sex tape?

68

Do you like your hair pulled during sex?

69

Do you enjoy the 69 position?

70

Have you ever been surprised by anything during sex?

Prize Page

The loser has to give the winner a foot massage for two minutes while telling the them all the ways they are amazing in bed. (If you don't know how they are in bed, then make it up.)

ROUND 8

71

Have you ever experienced an entire sexual encounter without ever lying down? If not, do you want to try?

72

Do you have any sexual secrets that would surprise me?

73

Have you ever reached orgasm in a shockingly quick amount of time?

74
Would you rather spank, or be spanked?

75
How do you feel about sleeping in the nude?

76
Phone sex: Hot or not?

__77__

Would you ever post a naked photo of yourself online?

__78__

Besides a bed or sofa, what's the next best piece of furniture to have sex on?

79

Have you ever worn a sexy Halloween costume? If not, would your wear one? What would you wear?

80

Is receiving nude photos hot, or not?

Prize Page

The loser has to gently tease and pleasure the winner using only their hands and fingertips for three minutes.

ROUND 9

81
What's the most sexually adventurous thing you've ever done?

82

Would you rather have sex in a bath or shower?

83

What was your earliest sexual thought or dream that you can remember?

84
Do you have any sexual fantasies that are embarrassing?

85
Do you have a sexual "bucket list?"

86

How often do you masturbate? When was the last time you did it?

87
Where were you the last time you masturbated?

88
Is there a sex position you don't like?

89

Is there a physical activity (other than sex) that turns you on?

90

Is it exciting to try new sexual positions or just awkward?

Prize Page

The loser has to orally pleasure the winner for two minutes in whatever way they wish.

ROUND 10

91
Would you have sex somewhere you might be caught?

92
Do you consider yourself "kinky" in the bedroom?

93
How would you rate yourself in bed?

94
Are massages sexually arousing, or do they just feel good?

95
Is watching porn with your significant other a turn-on?

96

Do you prefer initiating sex, or having your partner initiate?

97
What's the last "sexy" item you bought online or at an Adult store?

98
What turns you on more: flirting or foreplay?

99
Are there any uniforms you find sexy?

100
Are you turned on watching other people masturbate?

Prize Page

The winner of this round gets a sensual massage from the loser for five minutes.

ROUND 11

101
What's the hottest sexual experience you've ever had in your life?

102
Would you play dirty Truth or Dare in a group setting?

103
Is sex better at home or on vacation?

_104_
What's one kink or fetish that's a complete turn-off?

_105_
Do you like flavored lube or condoms?

106

What's hotter: No underwear, or sexy underwear?

107
Is sex better in good lighting, or in darkness?

108
Are sex clubs hot, or not?

109

What food(s) would you consider sexy to use in bed?

110

What do you like to do after sex?

Prize Page

The winner of this round gets to choose what they'd like the loser to do for the next one minute.

ROUND 12

111

Sex on a sandy beach: Hot or not?

112

How many times a week would you like to have sex?

<u>113</u>

Do you prefer it soft and gentle, or rough and passionate?

<u>114</u>

What do you feel is your best "sex move" in the bedroom?

_115_

Screamers in bed: Hot or not?

_116_

What's the sexiest thing you've ever read?

117
Would you perform in a porn video if you were paid enough?

118
Would you ever let someone watch you having sex?

_119_
Do you like being woken up with sex?

_120_
Leather, whips, and blindfolds: Hot or not?

Prize Page

Including this round, identify which player lost the most rounds and which player won the most rounds for the entire game.

The player who lost the most rounds needs to make one sexual fantasy come true for their partner. Winner's choice!

What's it going to be?

Spice up your love life even more, and explore all the discussion books for couples by J.R. James:

Love and Relationship Books for Couples

Would You Rather...? The Romantic Conversation Game for Couples (Love and Romance Edition)

Sexy Game Books for Couples

Would You Rather...? The Naughty Conversation Game for Couples (Hot and Sexy Edition)

Truth or Dare? The Sexy Game of Naughty Choices (Hot and Wild Edition)

Never Have I Ever... An Exciting and Sexy Game for Adults (Hot and Dirty Edition)

The Hot or Not Quiz for Couples: The Sexy Game of Naughty Questions and Revealing Answers

Pillow Talk: The Sexy Game of Naughty Trivia Questions for Couples

The Naughty Newlywed Game: A Sexy Game of Questions for Couples

Sexy Discussion Books for Couples

Let's Talk Sexy: Essential Conversation Starters to Explore Your Lover's Secret Desires and Transform Your Sex Life

All **THREE** *Let's Talk About...* sexy question books in one massive volume for one low price. Save now!

Let's Talk About... Sexual Fantasies and Desires: Questions and Conversation Starters for Couples Exploring Their Sexual Interests

Let's Talk About... Non-Monogamy: Questions and Conversation Starters for Couples Exploring Open Relationships, Swinging, or Polyamory

Let's Talk About... Kinks and Fetishes: Questions and Conversation Starters for Couples Exploring Their Sexual Wild Side

Change your sex life forever through the power of sexy fun with your spouse, partner, or lover!

www.sexygamesforcouples.com

Sexy Vacations for Couples
https://geni.us/Passion

ABOUT THE AUTHOR

J.R. James is a best-selling author who has a passion for bringing couples closer together and recharging their sexual intimacy. Erotic discussion is a powerfully sexy thing, and his conversation starter books have helped many couples reach new and sexually exciting heights in their relationships!

Sexy conversation with your partner is a magical, bonding experience. Through these best-selling question books, couples can find an easy way to engage in open and honest sexual discussion with each other. The result is a relationship that is both erotically charged and sexually liberating.

www.ingramcontent.com/pod-product-compliance
Lightning Source LLC
Chambersburg PA
CBHW071722020426
42333CB00017B/2359